MORE
ASSERTIVE
IN 30 DAYS

Ron Keller

CompCare® Publishers
2415 Annapolis Lane
Minneapolis, MN 55441

ISBN: 0-89638-294-X

Cover Design by Barry Littmann

Inquiries, orders and catalog requests should be sent to
CompCare Publishers
2415 Annapolis Lane
Minneapolis, MN 55441
Call toll free 800/328-3330
or 612/559-4800

BECOME MORE ASSERTIVE IN 30 DAYS

One Day at a Time.

Jane was raised to always put others' needs before her own. Her family expected her to wait on them and cater to them.

Jane went overboard to please her boss and allowed him too much freedom with her. She did not express her feelings to him. She did not tell him that she objected to the "sexist things" he asked her to do.

Jane was fed up with people taking advantage of her. One Monday morning, She looked in the mirror and determined to become more assertive immediately—again. On Monday and Tuesday, Jane walked around the office with her head up, shoulders back, and a hint of confidence in her voice. But no one noticed. By Wednesday, Jane had slipped back into her old patterns of behavior, such as accepting inappropriate assignments. She felt defeated and more hopeless than ever.

Becoming more assertive begins with where you are at this moment. It begins with what you do right now. Don't think about great plans for sudden change. Concentrate on the present.

Becoming more assertive is a gradual, day-by-day, moment-by-moment process. It begins with a simple awareness of the need to change. It grows with a longing to have a richer life by becoming all that you want to be. It is strengthened with courage and daily practice.

TODAY

Write on a slip of paper why you want to be more assertive, and list at least three things you need to change to meet your goal.

Boundaries

Shirley is learning how to assert herself by establishing appropriate boundaries for her personal and professional life. She also is learning how to let others know what her boundaries are.

Shirley has been learning to say no. In the past, Shirley rarely said no. She often found herself committing to things she didn't want to do, attending events she didn't want to attend, and giving away things she didn't want to give away. She assumed that if she ever said no, people would think less of her or like her less.

Shirley is finding that as she establishes and holds to her boundaries, others respect her more. The people she respects the most are her family members and friends who have clear boundaries.

Shirley is learning her limitations as well. She is letting people know that she is not "Super Mom" or "Super Girl Friday." When she needs help, she asks for it.

Shirley is learning the truth she discovered in a poster that reads:

There are two fundamental realities in life:

Number 1. There is a God.

Number 2. You are not she.

Shirley is finding freedom as she admits her limitations and clearly establishes and holds to her boundaries. She no longer feels the need to "play God."

TODAY

Practice saying no to someone today. It could be a salesperson, friend, family member, co-worker, whoever—if you don't want to buy it, do it, give it, or go to it, just say no.

Take Care of You

You can't give to others what you don't have yourself.

We love ourselves and others best when our own needs are met. To meet our needs, we need to take care of ourselves physically, mentally, emotionally, and spiritually. The better we feel about ourselves, the easier it is to positively assert ourselves.

The best way to demonstrate love for yourself is to take care of yourself. You are worth the time and energy that it takes to keep yourself together.

Ask yourself:

- Am I physically fit? Do I get enough exercise to keep my body toned? Do I eat healthful foods and get the nutrition I need to function at my best?

- Am I learning new things? Do I expose myself to new viewpoints?

- Are my emotional needs being met? Do I feel loved and appreciated by at least one other person? Do I have at least one person in whom I can confide?

- Are my spiritual needs being met? Do I know others who

share my beliefs about a power greater than myself?

What are your needs? How do you take care of yourself? These are different for each person. One truth is the same for all of us—we need to take care of ourselves. We all have needs that must be met.

To become more assertive involves knowing what you need, expressing those needs, and taking steps to be sure those needs are met.

TODAY

Learn one new thing today. Make a list of your needs. What need is most important to you? How can you see that it gets fulfilled?

Accept Yourself

I returned home to my wife and children after a five-day business trip. Before I could get my suitcase out of the trunk, my two-and-a-half-year-old son, Joshua, ran out of the house to meet me. Still wearing his bib and most of his lunch, he bolted toward me with outstretched arms and sticky fingers. I had on a white shirt, tie, and suit. One glance at him was all I needed to know that a hug from him would mean another trip to the dry cleaner.

Joshua didn't think about that. The thought of cleaning off the peanut butter and jelly before he hugged me never crossed his young mind. His only concern was to hug his dad. As I scooped him up in my arms, I knew Joshua's hug was worth more than the price of any dry cleaning bill.

Joshua knew that he was acceptable to me just as he was. He knew he didn't have to make any changes before I would embrace him. He knows now, twelve years later, that I still accept him and love him no matter what.

You are valuable just as you are. You are lovable just as you are. Will you accept yourself as you are?

Becoming more assertive means knowing yourself better. Being more assertive means accepting yourself just as you are.

TODAY

Repeat these words out loud several times today: I accept myself just as I am.

Assertiveness vs. Aggressiveness

"I am not to be disturbed," Carol barked at her receptionist. Carol slammed the door to her office, dumped her briefcase on her desk, and jammed the intercom button. "Where are the files I need?" Carol didn't wait for an answer. "I expect those files in here immediately or you will answer to me!"

Carol felt in total control as her receptionist rushed into the office and shakily placed the files on Carol's desk. Two weeks ago, Carol had completed an assertiveness-training course for managers.

Carol's mistake was confusing aggressiveness with assertiveness. There is a distinct difference between the two. The first is rooted in success at any cost; the latter is looking out for your own best interest in a socially responsible way.

Assertiveness is a way to let others know what we want while preserving our dignity and the dignity of those around us. Assertiveness means standing up for ourselves without fear. It is openly and honestly expressing our feelings and exercising our personal rights without infringing on the rights of others.

When someone is aggressive, she seeks to accomplish her goal even at the expense of others. To be aggressive is to make choices for others so you can get your own way. Aggressive behavior diminishes self-worth. It can be brutal, manipulative, threatening, and even violent. Carol missed the most important message of her assertiveness-training course. In her attempt to assert herself, she had become aggressive.

We must be careful to distinguish between assertiveness and aggressiveness. As we strive to be assertive, we may cross the line into aggression. If that happens, we need to recognize what we have done, take responsibility for our actions, and right any wrongs we may have committed. We needn't revert to our timid ways. Everyone makes mistakes. How we handle those mistakes is also part of our assertiveness training.

TODAY

List three personal rights you want to exercise.

Tell Your Story

Marilyn grew up in a home where no one talked about personal things. Her family did not express feelings. She was led to believe that being a "private person" was the only way to go through life.

To Marilyn, being a "private person" meant she could not reveal what life was really like for her. She was taught that to reveal her feelings would be to betray herself and her family.

"Let people wonder about who you are," her mother often said. "Keep them guessing."

Most of us long to be known for who we are. "I want at least one person to truly know me. And I want to know at least one other person," Marilyn told me several times in counseling sessions.

Contrary to what Marilyn learned, we become healthier as we tell our stories and share our lives. The various experiences of our lives have shaped and molded us. All that we have gone through has made us who we are today. How we respond to various situations, whether good or bad, builds character, strength, and endurance.

As we express these things to others, it helps to reinforce our significance to ourselves and others. Start telling your story to someone you know. Anecdotes and other tidbits from your life are good for boosting morale. A journal serves as a wonderful learning tool. It helps us pay attention to how we respond to various situations, people, and events. A journal also uncovers our weaknesses as well as our strengths.

TODAY

Tell a friend a part of your life story. Include concrete details or start keeping a journal. You will become more adept at journeling as you become comforatble doing it.

Stand Up for Yourself

In his profession, Jerry allowed himself to be pushed into administrative roles that he did not like. Despite feeling frustrated and unfulfilled he still performed well in these roles.

Through counseling, Jerry discovered that his temperament and personality were better suited for dealing with people rather than attending to administrative details. With this knowledge, Jerry told his company he needed to be placed in another role. His supervisors responded by moving him into the personnel department where he is now enjoying his role as a "people person."

Jerry's confidence and self-respect have increased since his job change. He is also more willing to assert himself in other areas of his life. All because he chose to take a stand for himself.

When you know and believe you have personal rights, you stand up for yourself. Set limits on your time and energy. Express yourself. Use your unique gifts and talents. Know your limitations. Decide what is too much or too little. Practice saying no. Don't hesitate to express, support, and defend your opinions.

Recognize that you have value and deserve to be treated with respect and dignity. Become an advocate for yourself. If you don't stand up for yourself, no one else will. You are the person best qualified to represent you. Learn to toot your own horn.

TODAY

As you talk to people today, be aware that your opinions and thoughts count. Don't be afraid to say what you mean.

Choose

For many years I have struggled with three significant areas of my life:

The first is my religious upbringing. I have chosen to accept some of the teachings I was given. I have rejected others.

The second is my ethnic background. I have chosen to adapt and integrate some of the good qualities that have come from my heritage. Others I have chosen to avoid.

The third is my childhood in the home of an alcoholic. I am learning about my tendencies to fix and help others. I have chosen to keep parts of those caring qualities and to reject other parts.

The power of choice is one of the greatest gifts we have received. We can choose to parent in one way or another. We can (sometimes) choose our lifestyle. We can choose our friends, church, social groups, home, and type of relationships we want to have. We can choose our moral and family values. We can choose to be victims or survivors. In one sense, we even can choose our own destiny.

We have unbelievable power and potential to include or exclude, gather or distribute, waste or save, move or stay. We are free to choose.

TODAY

What one thing in your life are you <u>not</u> doing that you would rather do? Ask yourself why. Give yourself an honest answer.

DAY 9

Resolving Conflict

Conflict occurs when two or more persons' ideas or desires come into opposition. Some people avoid conflict at any cost—sometimes sacrificing self-respect, moral values, and personal freedom. Others thoroughly enjoy the challenge that conflict brings. In fact, some people purposely create conflict to "spice up" life.

At some point in our lives we will face conflict. It cannot be avoided. Conflict can destroy our self-esteem or it can boost our self-confidence. Therefore, we need to know how to resolve conflict.

To resolve a conflict, we first must acknowledge that a conflict exists. We need to recognize the problem and honestly evaluate and define the situation.

Second, we must determine what is at stake. How much do we have invested in this conflict? What feelings are involved in the situation and toward the other party? What will each party lose if they concede to the other?

Third, we must take responsibility for our contribution to the conflict. If our action or inaction has added fuel to the conflict we need to remedy that.

Fourth, we should go directly to the other person involved in the conflict and calmly and clearly state the problem. We then can listen with an open mind to the other's point of view.

Finally, we must be willing to negotiate. Some conflicts are so minor that we may determine our position is not worth fighting for. Major conflicts that challenge our personal worth, moral beliefs, or personal rights require that we work to find acceptable alternatives in order to resolve conflict.

TODAY

Start small. Identify one minor conflict in your life and take one step toward resolving it.

Accept the Things You Cannot Change

"I won't live this way one more day," Charlene said. "I can't change John and I simply have to accept that."

Charlene wanted her marriage to work. She had invested everything in John and this marriage, but John's alcoholism had taken over their relationship. John was addicted and only he could change that, yet he was not ready to admit that he had a problem. He loved alcohol more than life itself. It was difficult for Charlene to admit this, but she finally did.

This kind of "tough love" is not easy, but often it is necessary to deal with difficult situations. After Charlene admitted that she could not change John she was better able to direct her energies to doing what was best for her children and herself. She couldn't change John, but she could change herself.

She experienced great freedom when she accepted what she could not change—John's alcoholism.

She found she had more energy to deal with other neglected areas of her life. There was a peace in letting go, in no longer fighting the inevitable.

We cannot change the world. We can, however, change one portion of the world—ourselves. More energy is wasted by people who cry over all that is wrong that they cannot change. Yet they fail to direct their strength toward fixing the things over which they do have power. It seems easier to complain about things beyond their control than to roll up their sleeves and do the things that they can.

Being assertive does not mean doggedly fighting a losing battle. To assert ourselves means not making choices for other people, no matter how much we love them. There is great hope and relief in letting go of things that are beyond our control. We become strong when we accept that we have done our best and move on.

TODAY

What one thing have you been trying to change that you need to let go? Employ "tough love" and let it go.

Change the Things You Can

Growing up around alcoholism could have handi-
capped me. Instead, I have made the best of my experiences and they have become a tremendous asset.

In my counseling and workshops, as I address
the real situations people deal with I swiftly get to the
heart of issues. My personal experiences have helped
me to be sensitive to the pain and problems others are
going through. I have the intuition needed to help
people.

I have accepted the impact alcoholism has on
my family. However, there are some things that I
don't have to accept about my family history. I can
change some things.

I have chosen not to act as a victim for the rest of
my life. I have been with sixty-year-olds who still cannot forgive and forget what their parents did or did
not do. These adults have not taken responsibility for
their own lives. They could go to their graves blaming
life's hardships on their parents.

Early in my life I subconsciously made some choices. I made a decision to accept what I could not change and to change what I could. As a child, I realized I couldn't change my dad or my circumstances, but I could change myself.

I have acknowledged my weaknesses. I no longer live in denial. I am empowered to change those areas of my life I can do something about.

Remember the serenity prayer: "God grant me the serenity to accept the things I cannot change, the courage to change the things I can, and the wisdom to know the difference." This kind of attitude makes all the difference.

TODAY

Write one thing that you can change in your life. Now think of one thing you can do today to move toward making that change.

Wisdom

A wise person not only has knowledge but also knows how and when to use that knowledge. Wisdom is extremely important when we face challenges. More than anything, we need wisdom to know which things we can change and which things we can't change.

Jim had invested twenty years of his life in working for a large corporation. In his career, seven bosses had come and gone. Each supervisor had a different temperament, personality, and management style. With each new boss, Jim showed flexibility, but he always braced himself for the worst.

His present boss is the most difficult of all. He drinks heavily. He is harsh and demanding. He has already managed to drive six of Jim's associates to other jobs.

Jim knows he will never change his boss. He therefore needs wisdom in knowing whether this is one of those situations in which he should stay or move on. He has counted the cost of staying, as well as the cost of quitting and seeking another job. Now he faces a major dilemma. Should he stay or quit?

When do we accept a situation the way it is? How do we know that we aren't supposed to keep working at changing things? How do we know that it's now time to change something that we have the ability to change? In all of these we need wisdom. Like Jim, each day, moment by moment, we need guidance and direction.

Wisdom is the ability to discern correctly which way to go and what to do. As Jim seeks wisdom through friends, family, intuition, and other sources, he will find it. Wisdom provides clarity.

TODAY

List three sources from which you can gain wisdom for your life.

DAY 13 ━━━━━━━━━━━━━━━━━
Intuition

Intuition. Most people have it. Few people act on it.

According to Webster, intuition is the immediate knowing or learning of something without the conscious use of reasoning. It is instantaneous apprehension.

Intuition is one of the gifts I appreciate most. The older I get, the more I use this wonderfully practical tool. And the more I use it, the more I trust it.

I can walk into a gathering of people and almost instantly ascertain the group's mood and focus. In counseling sessions I can quickly get a sense of what a person is going through and what is needed. This is not some unusual sixth sense. This is a common tool that most of us possess.

Exercising intuition is risky. We've been taught to act on well-reasoned conclusions; seldom do we act on our gut feeling.

Exercising intuition is acting in faith. It is the best of all assertiveness training. It develops faith in our ability.

Most people have ignored their intuition for so long, it seems impossible to revive it. It can be revitalized. Practice makes it reliable.

Moment by moment, we can train ourselves to listen to what our gut is telling us. If we are willing to act on the little intuitive signals our hearts give us, we will recognize more helpful signals.

Becoming more assertive involves the use of all of our gifts. One of the most significant of these gifts is intuition.

TODAY

What "gut feeling" did you ignore today? How could you respond differently the next time your intuition reveals something to you?

Focus on Today

A businessman was permitted to have one wish come true. After some thought, he wished for a newspaper dated two years into the future. Miraculously the paper was put into his hands. Turning to the stock reports, he made careful notes on the stocks that had shown unusual growth. He certainly would make a fortune.

Then out of curiosity he looked through the paper and, scanning the obituary column, found his name. The article listed heart attack as the cause of death, then spelled out in detail the funeral arrangements

Unlike the man in this story, we do not know our futures. We therefore should make today count. A day is a precious lifetime. One day at a time, we carefully live out the moments given to us.

Setting aside a few minutes at the end of each day to check your progress provides some important benefits:

1. It helps you prepare for tomorrow—by giving you a head start on the coming new day.

2. It helps you evaluate specific experiences that have helped or hindered your growth as you seek to become more assertive.

3. It helps you assess where you need to make changes. You can make changes day by day that you might not be able to do one week or month at a time.

Get in touch with yourself, your needs, and your desires. Assess daily how well you are expressing your needs.

TODAY

Take ten minutes this evening to ask yourself, How did I do today?

Self-expression

Experienced family specialists tell us that we learn three basic things in dysfunctional families: We learn to trust no one, to stuff our feelings, and to keep silent about who we really are. In other words, we give up self-expression.

Several barriers to self-expression exist. First, we may not express ourselves because we believe we don't have the right. If we have been taught to keep silent, it will be difficult for us to open up. We may fear how others will respond to us, or we may fear that we don't know how to properly express ourselves. Third, we may lack the skills needed for self-expression.

We need to express ourselves. To do so we must know what we feel. For many people, identifying their feelings is almost an impossibility. They have learned how to stuff, cover up, and medicate their feelings with addictions and activities.

Agnes was eighty-three years old when she redis-covered her feelings. For sixty years she had medicated her pain after her plans for marriage fell through when her fiancé abandoned her for another woman. Agnes had wept for days. Her tears turned to anger, her anger to bitterness and cynicism. Eventually the bitterness drove her to isolation. Agnes was unhappy, angry, and depressed.

When Agnes finally sought counseling her life changed. She revisited the terrible incident from her early years, admitted her feelings, and was finally able to release it.

We become healthy and strong when we face our past and express our present feelings. We need to find people we can trust with the intimate parts of our personality. Then we need to let people see who we really are.

Self-expression is best learned by doing. Identify your feelings, find someone you trust, and let them see who you are.

TODAY

Express your feelings to your spouse or closest friend.

DAY 16

Vision

I am a husband, father, writer, counselor, workshop leader, retreat leader, speaker, sailor, and theologian. My many roles sometimes can be confusing. I sometimes forget which of them I should be fulfilling at what time and to what extent. Without clear vision, I can easily flounder.

Your vision is ultimately what you want to accomplish in your lifetime. It is your driving desire, your main purpose and chief aim in life. It is that central cause or mission that motivates you and keeps you going. Your vision guides you as you make choices about the investment of your time, energy, and money. Without vision you lose heart, waste resources, and give up.

My vision can get hazy if I am not concentrating on the things I do best. When I lose sight of my vision, I get confused. My thinking gets fuzzy. My goals get obscured and I wander aimlessly.

I need clear vision. I frequently fight off the

temptation to do too many things. I need to have a clear, focused approach to what I really want to accomplish.

Vision helps you be more assertive. It helps you say, "This is what I am doing and why." Vision helps you avoid getting trapped by irrelevant, less urgent tasks and projects. It helps you define what you will be involved in and what you will avoid.

TODAY

What is your vision? Write it down. Be specific. Know what you need to do to and why.

DAY 17

Goals

Out of his passion to help hurting kids find a better life, Steve pursued a vision to own, manage, and operate a ranch for troubled kids. When he was a freshman in college, with the help of other adults, he began to chart a course that would help him fulfill his ultimate desires.

Steve knew what some of the obstacles might be. He leaned into those, accepting the fact that fulfilling his vision might be difficult.

One by one, Steve met his goals. Every summer, he worked at camps and resorts so he could learn more aspects of the management of such a facility. He saved money. He met with church and community leaders to help them understand his vision.

By the time he had graduated from college, Steve was working for a ranch that reaches out to troubled kids. He is slated to take over the management when the present owner retires.

Steve had a great vision. He also had clear goals.

He knew what he wanted and how to get it.

A vision needs clear goals to become reality. Goals are realistic, measurable, and specific. Your vision may be to become more assertive. Your goal could be to complete all activities in this book by the end of thirty days.

When you know what you want to accomplish, you can make choices that will lead you where you need to go. Know where you are going. Chart your course. Develop a "road map" of goals that will take you to your ultimate destination.

TODAY

List three goals that will help you become more assertive.

Self-image

Self-image comes from several sources.

Self-talk or internal dialogue is what we say to ourselves constantly—even in our dreams. Our self-talk reflects, in part, what we have been told by others. As we become more aware of what others tell us, we can choose to give ourselves new or different messages.

Family and friends, the people closest to us, have a great impact on how we view ourselves. Approval, criticism, rejection, support, or acceptance from family and friends can build up or destroy our self-image. As adults we can evaluate and then accept or reject the verbal and nonverbal messages of family and friends.

Society includes the media, our environment, and culture. All aspects of society give us messages of what is and is not acceptable. What we choose to value and identify with shapes our image of ourselves.

It is important to seek people, messages, and

and self-confidence.

Be aware of body posture. If you are sitting and the other person is standing, you may feel intimidated. It is best to be on an even level. Sit or stand without slouching or slumping. Hold your head high, shoulders back, and keep your hands relaxed. Avoid unnecessary fidgeting.

If you say something in a timid whisper you may be ignored. The tone, volume, and inflections of your voice add or detract from your verbal message. Practice speaking in a level, modulated tone.

These are just a few areas of communication. Most of us could stand some improvement in our communication skills. These basics can help us improve both our communication skills and our assertiveness skills.

TODAY

Pay special attention to nonverbal cues in your interactions today. What does the body language of the other person tell you? Work to send out positive, confident nonverbal cues.

Peer Influence

We influence all the people we encounter. They also influence us.

It's important to know whether their influence on us is positive or negative. It's also important that we try to be a positive influence on them.

I like being with people and am usually energized by being with them. Some individuals are like energy "gold mines" for me. My wife is usually one of these people. She is almost always positive and enthusiastic about life.

Other people, however, are a drain on me. For example, whenever I am in the presence of one particular person, I am troubled. I become pre-occupied, uncomfortable, and self-conscious. I do not feel good when I am around this person.

This individual is one of the few people that has such an immediate negative influence on me. I don't know if the way I react is my problem or the other person's. That doesn't even matter, because I know this indivdual is a good person.

For several years, I tried to understand why this acquaintance affects me so. I tried to make things better by going out of my way to get better acquainted and by trying to be especially nice. I did my best to "fix" the situation.

Now I've learned it's better to simply avoid each other.

Do you have someone like this in your life? Are you aware of who has a positive or negative impact on you?

TODAY

Make a list of the people who have a positive impact on you. Make a list of people who have a negative influence on you and decide what would be the best way to change the way such people affect you.

Ethics

My grandmother told me many times, "Always do the right thing." Doing the right thing always pays off. I reap what I sow. The measure that I use to give to others is the measure that is used for me.

Ethics are a set of principles used to determine right and wrong behavior. The "right thing" may mean different things to different people. Individuals determine personal ethical philosophies, but society also defines what is acceptable and unacceptable behavior.

When we do the right things we know they're right. When we do wrong we know it. We feel guilty and anxious to get things straightened out.

At all times, it is important for us to have a clear conscience. The clearer our conscience, the more assertive we can be. If our conscience is hazy, we will be less assertive. When we are feeling guilty or have done questionable things, we have little power, strength, or authority. If we have been deceitful, our life and voice lose integrity.

Taking the ethical high road is not a sign of weakness. It is, instead, a path to personal power.

TODAY

Make sure you have a clear conscience. Choose one person you have wronged. Call or write a letter to that person. Admit you're wrong and ask forgiveness for the offense.

Follow Your Passion

Jeff had a dilemma. He had a strong desire to serve as a missionary. His family approved, but only if he would accumulate enough savings to cover his financial needs. The problem: how much was enough?

Jeff spent years working in his family's business and saving money to please his parents. Then one day he had a heart attack and died. After burying their son, Jeff's family discovered that he had saved more than two million dollars. He never realized his dream.

What is it that you want to do? What do you feel called to do? What is the longing of your heart? These are questions about passion, your ultimate desire, your life mission.

We are strongest, and are most creative, productive, and assertive when we are in the flow of our passion.

Life is too short to pursue doing anything other than our passion. Too much is at stake. It is possible that some people could go through their entire lives doing everything except what they really want to do.

Are you following your calling? Are you doing what your heart is telling you to do? Do you feel impassioned by what you are doing?

Act on your innate desires. Set your passion free. Follow your heart.

TODAY

On a card, write down your greatest passion. Carry it with you and read it several times a day.

Support

People need someone who will stand behind them 100 percent. Someone who will support and encourage them during good times and bad. We all could benefit from assurance that, no matter what we did, at least one person would remain loyal to us. Such a person could be a friend, family member, spouse, or significant other.

Supportive friends and family build our self-esteem. They help us generate confidence in ourselves by reminding us of our assets, strengths, and gifts. They give us encouragement when we need it most. If we start to run ourselves down, a support person can lift us up. A support person can view us objectively and help keep us directed toward our vision.

It might be one person or a group of people who supports and encourages us. We all need a safe place where we can "come in for a landing," knowing that there we will be loved, appreciated, and accepted.

Surround yourself with people who will support

and encourage you. Get together with people who have positive, yet honest, things to say about you. Align yourself with people who have your best interest at heart. Invest yourself in relationships that are moving ahead, not backwards.

It is amazing that when we are valued by others we often learn to value ourselves more. Our self-confidence increases and we are able to stand up for what we believe.

TODAY

Thank someone for always being there for you. If you don't have a supportive person, make a list of people who might be able and willing to fill the role.

Compromise

A young couple had a good but often struggling marriage. Their worst times together centered on their mutual stubbornness. Ken wanted things done his way. Joann wanted them done her way. Neither was willing to give in to the other. Every issue was a major battle—from how to arrange the pillows on the couch to starting a family.

When tests showed that Joann was unable to conceive, eventually she accepted the news, then became adamant about adopting a child. Ken refused. "If we can't have our own children, then I don't want any," he repeatedly told Joann. As one negative encounter led to another, Joann and Ken found themselves growing further apart. Joann knew something had to give or their marriage would be destroyed.

Joann stimulated a tremendous change in their relationship when she admitted her stubbornness to Ken and expressed her love and concern for him. She told him, hard as it would be, that she would set aside for one year the idea of adopting children. She asked if Ken, in return, would re-evaluate their situation at that time.

Ken was overwhelmed by Joann's display of love. He realized what a great sacrifice she was making for the benefit of their marriage. Joann's actions helped him to realize just how selfish and pig-headed he had been. Compromise opened their hearts and eyes. Within one year they both had rationally agreed to adopt a child.

As we assert ourselves, as we stand up for our personal rights, we must be willing at times to negotiate. We should strive to have a mind-set that allows room for another's position.

We should seek win-win situations. Without being manipulated or violated, we can compromise and still get what we need and want out of a situation.

TODAY

Think of at least one situation in which you can compromise so both parties get what they want.

Recognize the Enemy

Most good football teams know and understand how the opposing team functions. They spend a great deal of time "scouting" and studying their opposition. In order to win, they know they need to understand and confront the tactics of their "enemy."

We may have an enemy, but ultimately, our worst enemy lives inside us. We are our own worst enemies. In many ways, we prohibit ourselves from becoming happier, more fulfilled people. We often do not trust what we feel. We are afraid to tap into our feelings and to trust our intuition.

We can easily identify our weaknesses but struggle with pinpointing our strengths. We minimize our capabilities, but emphasize the things we can't do well. Instead of remembering our successes, we dwell on our failures.

Many of us work hard to convince ourselves that we are not smart enough, attractive enough, talented enough. . . . We put limits on ourselves. We put the lid on our own capabilities and opportunities. We are our own worst critics and judges.

The enemy must be confronted. Reading books by positive-thinking authors such as Dr. Norman Vincent Peale (*The Power of Positive Thinking*) will help us deal with the enemy within. Using affirming statements about ourselves throughout the day and speaking positively will help us become more assertive. Other enemies will seem less threatening as we conquer the enemy within.

TODAY

Pay special attention to your self-talk. Make a point to give yourself affirming, uplifting, positive messages.

Discipline

Doug has been overweight most of his life. He has tried every diet imaginable, but none has worked. He admits that he has difficulty following through on his commitment to exercise, eat the proper foods, and avoid his favorite desserts. Doug is the first to acknowledge that what he truly lacks is discipline.

Discipline will help Doug with his problem. It is not the only problem, but it is an important component. Doug feels his lack of discipline and consequent weight problem have adversely affected his confidence and self-esteem.

Discipline is training that produces positive patterns of behavior. It can be physical, mental, or spiritual. It can involve great quantities of time or a few minutes a day. Discipline varies with each person. For some a disciplined life comes easily; for others it requires great effort.

Discipline offers many advantages. Discipline helps us develop habits and behaviors that will make us stronger. Physical discipline can increase stamina, endurance, and strength. Mental discipline increases knowledge, expands our ability to comprehend, and improves interpersonal communication. Spiritual discipline can help us to become more at peace with ourselves and more hopeful about the future.

As we become more disciplined, we feel we are better able to handle all areas of our lives. Our confidence in our abilities increases. We are more aware of our potential and we are encouraged to press ahead.

TODAY

Make a list of the areas of your life in which you are well disciplined.

DAY 28

Full Potential

Scientists believe that human beings use less than ten percent of their potential brain power. Considering that ninety percent of our brain is not being used, it is amazing how much we can actually accomplish. Even knowing that we could do more, few of us are inspired to seek new ways to increase our potential brain power.

We are gifted people. We were created with certain gifts and talents. These can be used for our own fulfillment or for the benefit of others. Still, many of us fail to use our talents. When our gifts remain unused, not only we but others are deprived of what we have to offer.

We all have some things that we do well: skills, talent, ability that seems to come naturally—with little effort on our part. Discovering these gifts is crucial and is the first step toward fully using our potential. We should not settle for just "getting by" but should strive to excel in all areas of our lives.

We should listen to those closest to us. Often they can help us recognize the potential we take for granted. We need to take an honest look at ourselves and reflect on the accomplishments we have made. We should press for the full use of our potential.

We have been given gifts and talents to use to the fullest. We also possess the strength to do what needs to be done. It is not necessary to take shortcuts or search for the easy road. We can and should aim for quality—excellence!

As we strive to make full use of our potential, we will see how much we truly have to offer. We can take pride in our gifts and talents and accept them as a unique expression of who we are.

TODAY

Which talent that you possess is lying unused? What could you do today to unleash its potential?

Self-Confidence

Confidence is a feeling of assurance. Self-confidence is a feeling of assurance and trust in oneself. It is that trust in our ability to do and be. A confident person enjoys and appreciates herself. A confident person is proud of what she has done and the potential that is within her.

When a person is confident she has no problem being herself. She is able to share herself with others. She does not hesitate to express her needs and wants to others. She knows what her personal rights are and is aware of her abilities and limitations. She is not afraid to say no. She makes healthy choices and has a clear vision of where she is headed.

A person with self-confidence can enjoy being alone and enjoys spending time with others. She understands the necessity of solitude and fellowship in her life. She is interdependent. She needs people, but not compulsively. She has strong ties but is not codependent. She can work in collaboration with others, but she is also fully capable of functioning on her own.

A self-confident person appreciates positive feedback as well as constructive criticism. Her self-esteem is not based on what others think or say about her. She is content with her value and significance as a human being.

The self-confident person is honest. She is comfortable with herself. She is balanced, healthy, and stands on a solid foundation. She feels good about herself regardless of whether others support her or not. She is committed, above all else, to being herself.

TODAY

Step out into the world with confidence.

Relax

The wise, aging spiritual director said to one of her counselees, "Most people take life too seriously. They are consumed with meeting deadlines and goals. Their lives are filled with anxiety and activity. People will live longer and better if they will learn to relax."

The life of the average child is one of carefree days, adventure, and fun. Children enjoy life. They trust. They laugh. They take each day and adventure as it comes.

Inside every adult is a child that longs to toss aside the schedules, deadlines, and responsibility— an inner child who simply wants to kick back and relax. As adults we are often uptight about life. We forget to live. We have no time to enjoy a sunset, take a leisurely stroll, play a game, or enjoy the company of those we love.

We need to slow down, unwind, play. Leisure is a good way to recharge our batteries. Daily stresses, conflict, and routines zap our strength. We can suffer physical illness and mental anguish. We may become irritable, depressed, or frustrated. After a reprieve our mind is sharper, our body is rested, and our attitude is more positive. We may have a surge of energy, creativity, and productivity.

We need to relax. We need to laugh. We need to be kids once in a while.

TODAY

Take off your watch. Hide your calendar. Eat when you're hungry. Sleep when you are tired. Don't plan a thing. Relax and enjoy life.

Perfect Gifts for Any Occasion